Every Day is a Gift

THIRTY DAYS TO A MORE THANKFUL YOU
(HOW TO GROW IN GRATITUDE)

BRIDGET A. THOMAS

Scripture quotations are taken from the Holy Bible, New Living Translation, copyright ©1996, 2004, 2015 by Tyndale House Foundation. Used by permission of Tyndale House Publishers, Inc. Carol Stream, Illinois 60188. All rights reserved.

Visit the author's website at www.bridgetathomas.com.

Cover design and artistic design by Stacey Witkowski, www.StaceyWitkowski.com.
Edited by Stacey Witkowski, www.StaceyWitkowski.com.
Formatted by Jen Henderson, www.wildwordsformatting.com.

Disclaimer: The author of this book is not a licensed counselor. This book is not intended as a guide to diagnose any medical or psychological issues. If expert assistance is needed, please seek help from a health-care provider or licensed counselor. This work is sold with the understanding that neither the author nor the publisher are held responsible for a perceived negative outcome as a result of the contents of this book.

ISBN-13: 978-1-7322020-0-9
ISBN-10: 1-7322020-0-1

Introduction

Welcome! I am so glad you are here. If you are like me, then maybe you struggle with complaining. Or maybe many days you don't want to get out of bed. Or maybe life seems a bit insipid at times. If any of this rings true, then this book is for you.

I will walk you through my own journey in finding joy through gratitude. I will show you the things that got me started on this path, and how I persevered. And I will also help you unlock the door to your own gratitude, which will in turn bring you true contentment.

This book came to life on one blustery day when everything seemed to go wrong. Nothing major. Just a lot of little things. I spilled coffee on my clothes as I got in the car to head to work. Then, since it was still dark, I ran over debris in the road. I knocked my water bottle over on my desk - twice. I missed a meeting that was on my calendar. The list goes on...

I was so glad to head home that day and put it all behind me. But since I have a one-hour commute, I had plenty of time to pray on my way home. And I felt like God was asking me an important question. "Will you give thanks during the rough times?" I must confess that my attitude that morning had not been pretty, and I needed that reminder. And that was when I started the gratitude challenge. In the beginning, I walked through it on my own. After taking the journey myself, I thought it would be beneficial to share it with others. And the response was so positive, I decided to share it with all of you.

This book is broken down into thirty short passages. The idea is to read one each day for thirty days. At the end of each day we have a time of reflection. This section will help you overcome any struggles that might be holding you back from finding gratitude. And at the end of each day, I will ask you to write down five things that you are thankful for. But please note that it is best to do that particular step each night. (We will talk about why this is important later on.) So if you read each passage in the morning, please hold off on writing down the five things you are thankful for until the evening. Unless you want to write down things that you are thankful at both times of the day. There would be no harm in doing that.

Now is the time to see for yourself how gratitude can change your life. I am excited to see what God will teach us through this journey. When you complete this challenge, please tell me how it went at www.bridgetathomas.com. I would love to hear from you. Now let's get started!

Part 1

Getting Started
with Gratitude

Day 1

Whatever is good and perfect is a gift coming down to us from God our Father, who created all the lights in the heavens. He never changes or casts a shifting shadow.

— James 1:17

"Every day is a gift!" Since 2012 I have had that phrase as part of my email signature. That was the year when a friend from college died of sarcoma. It was only one week after Jennifer's thirty-fourth birthday. She left behind a husband, a two-year-old daughter, loving parents, and countless friends. Jennifer had such a beautiful heart. She was always smiling, and always thinking of others.

I've often asked God why this had to happen. Why do some get to live and others die? Why would someone so young lose the battle? Why did a toddler have to lose her mom? Why would such a sweet spirit be chosen? This side of heaven, I might never know the answers to these questions.

Piercing moments in life like this can change us. Sometimes they will make us more resentful. But they don't have to. We can choose to use these moments to cling to God, and ultimately to make us stronger.

When my friend died, this made me more thankful for Jesus. Why? Because Jesus gives me hope that I will see my friend again one day. And in the meantime, I want to cherish what she didn't get - extra time on this earth. Extra time to love my family. Extra time to be a blessing to others. I want to remember that every day is a gift from God.

Every day is a gift!

Daily Reflection

Is there a defining moment in your life that has changed your perspective?

_____

_____

_____

_____

_____

Did it crush your outlook on life or did it cause you to treasure life?

_____

_____

_____

_____

_____

Evening Reflection

Write down five things that you are thankful for.

_____

_____

_____

_____

_____

_____

_____

_____

Day 2

Don't be afraid, for I am with you. Don't be discouraged, for I am your God. I will strengthen you and help you. I will hold you up with my victorious right hand.

– Isaiah 41:10

I had been sick for a couple of weeks and I was desperate for some sleep on one particular Saturday. So when I woke up with a cough early that morning, I was not happy. I got up so that I wouldn't disturb my husband and went to the guest bedroom. But I admit that I was grumbling along the way. "Why can't I just get some sleep? Why does this have to happen to me?" Yes, I was being a bit dramatic, I know!

I laid my head on the pillow, having a pity party. Then the next thing I knew, I was getting up around nine o'clock. That is unheard of in our house. I couldn't believe I slept so late. My husband and I are both early risers. And in general when one of us gets up, the other does as well.

And then I knew that the cough that woke me up which I was grumbling about, was in reality a blessing in disguise. If I had stayed in bed, I would have gotten up the same time my husband did, hours earlier. I learned that day the importance of starting each day with a grateful heart, rather than a grumbling heart. In all honesty, I believe the Lord used this small incident to show me the importance of disciplining my mind. It is important to do this all throughout the day. But I found that when the day begins, in particular, we need to start it off on the right foot.

Otherwise, we run the risk of the day spiraling downhill from there. Let me give you an example. One morning as I drove to work, I was annoyed at some of the drivers on the road. Nothing major, just some people who seemed to be inconsiderate. I was waiting to make a left-hand turn, but there was a truck coming from the other direction. Well, the truck wound up making a left-hand turn as well, but he didn't have his blinker on. So I could have gone, if I had known. And this particular morning, I let that get under my skin. Then only a few moments later, I hit an armadillo. You might think this was a coincidence, but I felt God reminding me that we should be slow to anger (James 1:19).

So first thing in the morning, try to send your thoughts in the right direction. Make it a ritual while you are brushing your teeth. Put some sort of triggers on your bathroom mirror. This might sound silly, but it works. At my house we currently have four Bible verses, one prayer, and an "I love you" note on our bathroom mirror!

Start each day with a grateful heart.

Daily Reflection

Can you think of a time when things didn't go your way, but it really turned out to be a blessing?

_____

_____

_____

_____

_____

What triggers can you put on your bathroom mirror to remind yourself to start the day with a grateful heart?

_____

_____

_____

_____

_____

Evening Reflection

Write down five things that you are thankful for.

Day 3

Jesus spoke to the people once more and said, "I am the light of the world. If you follow me, you won't have to walk in darkness, because you will have the light that leads to life."

– John 8:12

This new path wasn't easy. I discovered that I had fallen into a habit of complaining all throughout the day. To be honest, if I stopped to think about it, I didn't like complaining. It made me feel worse about whatever was bothering me. And I am sure that it brought down those around me as well. And I knew that God didn't like it either. In the Old Testament we can see how God feels about complaining.

In Numbers 11:1 it says, "Soon the people began to complain about their hardship, and the Lord heard everything they said. Then the Lord's anger blazed against them, and he sent a fire to rage among them, and he destroyed some of the people in the outskirts of the camp."

YIKES! Reading these words fills me with remorse and causes me to deeply regret my griping. But how do we change, when it is something that is so ingrained in us? Start by praising God for the good things in your life. Look around for a moment and you will see so many blessings. The truth is, there are always tons of things that God does for us. Every single day. But we often overlook the good things, and concentrate on the bad things. Just like the Israelites in the desert, who were delivered from slavery, yet they still chose to complain.

As I walked through the day, looking for good things, I would remind myself - The world already has enough complainers. Let's spread light by practicing gratitude.

One habit that helped me was to write down things that I was thankful for. Putting pen to paper seemed to be more concrete than just thinking about them. It helped me to take notice of the good things in life. If we merely take a glance, we will be quick to move on to some other distraction and potentially lose the awesomeness of it all. And I feel it is critical to write down those things at the end of the day. Reflect on your day and take note of the good things that occurred during that day. Even if you had a bad day, you will see that some good things still happened. I mentioned before that we should start our day with a grateful heart. But it is just as important to end the day with a grateful heart. Having a content or peaceful spirit while you drift to sleep will have lasting effects on your attitude in the long run. And it will help you to wake up with a better outlook the following morning.

That is why at the end of each day, I ask you to write down five things you are thankful for. When I began this journey, I would write down ten things each day. But I decided to go easy on you!

The world already has enough complainers.
Let's spread light by practicing gratitude.

Daily Reflection

Do you have a habit of complaining and are you willing to change that today?

_____

_____

_____

_____

_____

Do something fun today which will help you look at the brighter side of life.

_____

_____

_____

Evening Reflection

Write down five things that you are thankful for.

Day 4

Then Jesus said to the disciples, "Have faith in God. I tell you the truth, you can say to this mountain, 'May you be lifted up and thrown into the sea,' and it will happen. But you must really believe it will happen and have no doubt in your heart. I tell you, you can pray for anything, and if you believe that you've received it, it will be yours. But when you are praying, first forgive anyone you are holding a grudge against, so that your Father in heaven will forgive your sins, too."

— Mark 11:22-25

When I started down this path, I thought everything would miraculously change in my life. But it wasn't that easy. I still got stuck sometimes. I still seemed to have some hang-ups in life. I still felt negative feelings. So I took some time to examine what the problem was and God led me to Mark 11:22-25.

Let's examine this in two parts. The first half explains that we need to really and truly believe, deep down, that we will receive what we asked for. This might be difficult to do, especially if we are asking for something that seems immense to our human minds. In the past, when I prayed to God about my dream of writing, I would often follow it up with, "if it's Your will." I added those few extra words as a subconscious way of saying that it would never happen. Publishing a book seemed like such a huge and almost outlandish idea. But here is the key - the things that seem enormous to us, are tiny to God. It is nothing for Him to accomplish the things in life that we feel are mammoth in size. Hand your epic dreams over to God and you will be surprised at the results.

The second half of the Bible passage at the top of the page talks about forgiveness. This is a tough one. I believe that many people have a tendency to hold grudges, myself included. When other people hurt us, it can be hard to let it go. Years later we still relive the scene in our minds, and we get riled up all over again as though it just happened. But according to this Bible verse, forgiveness is something we must master if we want God to answer our prayers. If you are holding any grudges, please let it go today, and you will feel a weight lifted. When God pointed me to this passage, I took time to go through every single person I knew and I said to myself, "I forgive them." Even if I couldn't think of any reason for being upset with that person, I felt it was best to do this just in case I held a hidden grudge in my subconscious that I wasn't aware of. After I went through this process, I felt lighter, happier, and more at peace.

If you are holding any grudges, please let it go today, and you will feel a weight lifted.

Daily Reflection

When you pray for something, do you really believe that you will receive what you asked for? Why or why not?

_____

_____

_____

_____

_____

Are you holding any grudges today? Will you consider letting them go for your own peace of mind?

_____

_____

_____

_____

_____

Evening Reflection

Write down five things that you are thankful for.

Day 5

Dear brothers and sisters, when troubles of any kind come your way, consider it an opportunity for great joy. For you know that when your faith is tested, your endurance has a chance to grow. So let it grow, for when your endurance is fully developed, you will be perfect and complete, needing nothing.

— James 1:2-4

Once I started looking around for good things in my life, it helped me to feel better on the inside. I could feel an inner peace beginning to form. But then things seemed to change on the outside as well. It didn't feel like so many things were going wrong. And I started to see all the things that were going right.

When we had to obtain a new refrigerator, I saw how everything magically lined up with the purchase and delivery. When we needed to acquire a new water pump, I was amazed that someone came and fixed it within hours. When our vacuum broke and we went to the store to exchange it, I couldn't believe that we actually received money back because the vacuum was on sale that day.

I began to realize that practicing gratitude helps us to focus on all that we have, rather than what we lack. As you can see, there were still a number of things that were "wrong." We are always going to have issues to deal with in life. But in the past, I would have been grumbling about the refrigerator, the water pump, and the vacuum. But now, I was focusing on the way God paved a smooth path in each case. Gratitude helped open my eyes in a new way. I couldn't believe all the things that I had been missing in life. Once I let gratitude get deep into my soul, it was like a whole new world had been presented to me.

Practicing gratitude helps us to focus
on all that we have, rather than what we lack.

Daily Reflection

Can you name a time when something was broken in your life (literally or figuratively), but God still worked behind the scenes to help correct it?

Looking back on this broken thing, do you think that might help change your perspective today and in the future?

_____

_____

_____

_____

_____

Evening Reflection

Write down five things that you are thankful for.

_____

_____

_____

_____

_____

_____

_____

Day 6

And let the peace that comes from Christ rule in your hearts.
For as members of one body you are called to live in peace.
And always be thankful.

– Colossians 3:15

It can be very difficult to keep up with all the things that we "should" be doing. My husband often hears healthy tips on the radio that he shares with me. Eat black pepper - every day. Eat pineapple - every day. Eat two bananas - every day. And so on. If we ate all the things that we were told to eat, we would explode. And then there is the exercising we should be doing. Get ten thousand steps a day, work on muscle tone, do some breathing exercises, stretch every day. It can all be so overwhelming.

But there is one change that you can make in your life that is guaranteed to help in all other areas. And that is practicing gratitude. Gratitude is medicine for the soul. Countless studies have shown that gratitude can help you improve your outlook on life and boost your health as well.

And this was something I was seeing in my own life as well. The more I practiced gratitude, the happier I felt. It wasn't always easy. In the beginning I needed triggers to keep my mind focused. It might sound strange, but one thing that worked for me was to wear a rubber band around my wrist. When I saw the rubber band, I would remember that I was supposed to be focusing on gratitude. I had to be intentional about concentrating on gratitude, and remind myself all throughout the day. I also kept a notebook on my bathroom sink, to remind myself to write down the things I was grateful for each evening. But when I was diligent about it, it paid off, and over time I had more joy in my life.

Gratitude is medicine for the soul.

Daily Reflection

Over the past few days of this journey, have you felt happier when writing down things you were grateful for?

_____

_____

_____

_____

_____

What triggers can you use to remind yourself throughout the day to focus on gratitude?

_____

_____

_____

_____

_____

Evening Reflection

Write down five things that you are thankful for.

_____

_____

_____

_____

_____

_____

_____

_____

_____

Day 7

Always be full of joy in the Lord. I say it again - rejoice!

– Philippians 4:4

When I was a child, I was in the hospital a number of times. In all honesty, I can't even tell you how many times. It was horrible. I had a condition that was very scary, for myself and my family. We never knew when I would have a reoccurrence and this left us all on edge for years. We even had a couple of hospital visits while out of town on vacation. Everywhere we went, we had to wonder if I would be ok. I felt trapped and I am sure my family did too. To say it was not fun, is an understatement.

Then one day my sister prayed for me. And after that? I was fine. It never happened again. We never had to call the paramedics again. I never had to go to the hospital again. My family didn't live on edge anymore. We could go out without worrying about what might happen.

While this period of my life was very unpleasant, it did teach me something - there is always something to be thankful for. Now looking back, I can still be thankful. I can be thankful that I was never seriously harmed in the process. I can be thankful that I am well now. I can be thankful that I had a loving family who supported me. I can be thankful for doctors, nurses and medicine that help millions of people every single day. I can be thankful for healing. I can be thankful for miracles. And I can be thankful for my sister's prayer.

There is always something to be thankful for.

Daily Reflection

Can you think of a time in your life that you would not like to repeat?

_____

_____

_____

_____

_____

Looking back on the situation, is there anything you can give thanks for now?

_____

_____

_____

_____

_____

Evening Reflection

Write down five things that you are thankful for.

_____

_____

_____

_____

_____

_____

_____

_____

Part 2

Gratitude Starts
on the Inside

Day 8

Then I will praise God's name with singing, and I will honor him with thanksgiving.

– Psalm 69:30

I used to dread getting up in the morning. Most days everything in life seemed just plain hard. When I turned off the alarm clock, right away I would have unhappy thoughts floating in my head. I dreaded work, I dreaded people, and I dreaded life in general.

Fortunately, I would often realize I was having bitter thoughts before my feet hit the floor. I am one of those people whose mind starts spinning as soon as I wake up. So I started telling God that I was sorry to have such an acidic tone first thing in the morning. And I tried to turn it around. I thanked God for my amazing husband. I thanked God for another day on earth. I thanked God for the good job I had. I thanked God for great coworkers. By the time I made it to the powder room, I thanked God for indoor plumbing!

Some mornings I would wonder, what if God took away the things that I didn't seem to appreciate. That was a scary thought. And it made me regret the times when I had a thankless attitude. God gives us all so much every day. But too often, we take it all for granted. I know I did.

And to be honest, I didn't want to live in a state of dread anymore. It wasn't fun. Life shouldn't be lived that way. I wanted my days to be filled with joy. And that's what God wants for His children too. But finding happiness and gratitude starts on the inside. So that was when I decided to find the key that would turn things around. That was when I decided to start living with a spirit of gratitude, each and every day.

Finding happiness and gratitude starts on the inside.

Daily Reflection

What is your thought pattern first thing in the morning? Are you a morning person or a grumbler?

_____

_____

_____

_____

If it's the latter, how can you change it?

_____

_____

_____

_____

_____

Evening Reflection

Write down five things that you are thankful for.

_____

_____

_____

_____

_____

_____

_____

_____

Day 9

...We capture their rebellious thoughts and teach them to obey Christ.

– 2 Corinthians 10:5

I have a personal cheerleader. Someone who tells me what a great job I have done. For the most part it pertains to my physical activity. If I burned a set amount of calories in the day, my cheerleader is there uplifting me. If I stood up for part of my day, instead of sitting the whole time, I have cheers coming my way. If I am slacking a little, I am told that I can do it. This personal cheerleader is my smartwatch.

It's nice to know I have someone in my court. But I believe that we should start a habit of being our own cheerleaders. I don't mean that we should puff ourselves up to the point of conceit. But the truth is that most of us tend to talk about ourselves in a negative way. We beat ourselves up over mistakes. We defeat ourselves with our own pessimism.

Personally, that was one thing I had to work on in this journey, my own negativity towards myself. Throughout the day, when I noticed a self-deprecating thought, I would pull the brakes on the runaway train in my head. Then I would remind myself, "You are perfect and whole in Jesus." This akes a lot of time, patience, and perseverance. But it is possible. And before long, you will notice yourself becoming happier.

Once we start expressing more gratitude, our eyes will not only be opened to all the goodness around us; but we will also see more goodness within ourselves too. We will be friendlier toward the person we see in the mirror. And that helps us to be nicer to those around us.

You are perfect and whole in Jesus.

Daily Reflection

Do you participate in a lot of negative self-talk? What are some of the things you say about yourself?

_____

_____

_____

_____

_____

Does this align with God's Word? If not, how can you change it?

_____

_____

_____

_____

Evening Reflection

Write down five things that you are thankful for.

_____

_____

_____

_____

_____

_____

_____

Day 10

For the Lord is good. His unfailing love continues forever, and his faithfulness continues to each generation.

– Psalm 100:5

Thanksgiving - a holiday in the United States when one day out of the year the whole country seems to be in harmony. We all get up in the morning, looking forward to the parade on television, and putting our turkeys in the oven. We are happy that we will get to spend the day with our loved ones. From coast to coast, families gather around to enjoy good food and fellowship. How amazing that we have a holiday dedicated towards giving thanks.

But gratitude should be something we practice all throughout the year, not just on one day in late November. If you are from the United States, then you know that this state of accord doesn't last. Later that evening the Black Friday sales start. And now the people who were filled with gratitude might be found in a fist fight just so that they could be the first in line for a deal on a hot new toy, television, or video game. Ironic.

It is heartbreaking really, how quick we are to forget the feelings we had on Thanksgiving as we sat at the table with ar loved ones. But I would love to see this change. And maybe you agree? While we might not be able to change everyone, we can change our own attitudes by practicing gratitude beyond that one day. And we can pray that this in turn will have an impact on those around us. Too often we let those around us bring us down. But we have to learn to be the light that brings other people up. It is not always easy. Trust me, I know. I am one of those people that is easily affected when I am surrounded by negativity. But from now on, I am going to change that. And I hope you will join me. We get to decide how we will feel. So today let's choose to be happy.

While we might not be able to change everyone, we can change our own attitudes by practicing gratitude.

Daily Reflection

What is your favorite holiday and why?

Will you join me on this mission? Are you willing to try to change your own attitude today?

_____

_____

_____

_____

_____

Evening Reflection

Write down five things that you are thankful for.

_____

_____

_____

_____

_____

_____

Day 11

Great is his faithfulness; his mercies begin afresh each morning.

– Lamentations 3:23

I love to read in my spare time. Some books leave more of an impression than others. One of those books is called *Same Kind of Different as Me*, which has also been made into a movie. This is a true story and quite a fascinating tale of a homeless man, Denver Moore, and a well-to-do couple, Ron and Deborah Hall, who became friends.

There are certain passages in the book that I hope to never forget. One day when Deborah was helping feed the homeless, she had an encounter with one particular man. The words below were written by her husband, Ron.

> *This man ate from garbage cans, an unpleasant truth you knew automatically if you had a nose. His beard was matted with dried vomit and the remnants of his last few meals, and he reeked so strongly of booze that it seemed he might explode if someone got too close and struck a match.*
>
> *Here was a man whose life seemed disposable. Yet he found a reason to smile. Drawn to him, Deborah offered*

him a plate of home-cooked food and a prayer. Then, truly puzzled, she asked him, "Why are you so happy?"

"I woke up!" he replied, eyes twinkling in his haggard face, "and that's reason enough to be happy!"

Deborah rushed home to tell me what he'd said, as though she'd been given a treasure that needed to be deposited immediately in my memory bank. From that day on, three words—"We woke up!"—were the first to come out of our mouths, a tiny prayer of thanksgiving for something we'd always taken for granted, but that a derelict had had the wisdom to see as a blessing fundamental to all others.[1]

If you woke up today, then you already have one thing to be thankful for.

Daily Reflection

Does reading this story give you a new perspective on life?

Take a moment to thank God for another day on this earth.

_____

_____

_____

_____

_____

Evening Reflection

Write down five things that you are thankful for.

_____

_____

_____

_____

_____

_____

_____

_____

Day 12

I thank and praise you, God of my ancestors, for You have given me wisdom and strength. You have told me what we asked of you and revealed to us what the king demanded.

– Daniel 2:23

There are many people in the Bible who I like to read about. So many great stories of faith for us to learn from. One of those is Daniel. Many of us have heard about Daniel and the lions' den. During this time, Daniel was living in Babylon where the king passed a law stating that if there was anyone who did not pray to the king himself, they would be thrown into the lions' den.

Daniel 6:10 says, "But when Daniel learned that the law had been signed, he went home and knelt down as usual in his upstairs room, with its window open toward Jerusalem. He prayed three times a day, just as he had always done, giving thanks to his God."

Two of the king's men reported to the king that even though this law was passed, Daniel still prayed to God. The king liked Daniel and he was troubled when he learned about this. He tried to think of a way to save Daniel, but in the end he decided not to go back on his word.

So Daniel was thrown into the lions' den. Early the next morning the king hurried to check on Daniel and found that he was still alive. God had sent an angel to shut the lions' mouths. The king was so overjoyed that he ordered everyone in his kingdom to fear the God of Daniel.

How amazing that God not only saved Daniel, but even changed the heart of this king. But one key to this story is Daniel's faith and thanksgiving. I think Daniel knew a secret - complaining makes us feel bitter, while gratitude makes us feel better.

When trouble comes knocking on our doors, do we give thanks, like Daniel did? In all likelihood, the answer is no. Most humans have a tendency to complain about our problems. But Daniel was different. Even when the worst was knocking at his door, Daniel still gave thanks to God.

Complaining makes us feel bitter,
while gratitude makes us feel better.

Daily Reflection

When trouble comes your way, do you immediately hand it over to God? Or do you live in fear and anxiety? Or do you run to your friends and complain about the problem?

_____

_____

_____

_____

If you are one of the latter two, take a moment to ask God to
help you be better about turning your troubles over to Him.

_____

_____

_____

_____

Evening Reflection

Write down five things that you are thankful for.

_____

_____

_____

_____

Day 13

Three things will last forever - faith, hope, and love - and the greatest of these is love.

— 1 Corinthians 13:13

86,400 seconds. That is what we get each and every day. What will you do with your 86,400 seconds today? It sounds like a lot of time. And yet the twenty-four hours seem to slip by so fast. There is always so much to do. Sometimes I wish God gave me more than two hands so I could accomplish more.

My husband often has a good laugh when I am cleaning up the table after dinner. I try to carry all of the dishes, cups, and utensils back into the kitchen in one pass. I pile everything up and have to be extra careful to balance it all.

In moments like those I know that God knew exactly what He was doing when He gave us only two hands. We already try to take on too much in life as it is. And if we were given the chance, we would take on even more.

So we have to learn to portion out our time well. And we have to make sure we allow time for the treasures in our lives. Things like loving our families and giving thanks to God.

If you are like me, perhaps you get tunnel vision. You get so focused on your projects and to-do lists that you don't want to stop and take time for matters of the heart. But when it's all said and done, God and our families are the things that matter the most.

Of course we still have to go to work, do the laundry, mop our floors, and so on. But those things will always be there. And we can't let our focus on them take away from our focus on the things that matter most.

What will you do with your 86,400 seconds today?

Daily Reflection

Do you often try to take on too much? Do you get irritated when the stress of it all threatens to topple over?

_____

_____

_____

_____

_____

Will you take time today to breathe, to love your family, and to give thanks to God?

_____

_____

_____

_____

_____

Evening Reflection

Write down five things that you are thankful for.

_____

_____

_____

_____

_____

_____

_____

_____

_____

Day 14

Seek the Kingdom of God above all else, and live righteously, and he will give you everything you need.

– Matthew 6:33

When, God, when? When will we be out of debt? When will I publish my book? When will I finally stop living as though I am trapped, even though You set me free? When will I ever get over this? When will I get that job I have been wanting? When will I get married? When will we get a new home? When will we have children?

Do you ever ask God questions like these? I do. More often than I care to admit. Everybody's "when" questions will look different. But most of us fall into this trap.

In times like these, we need to remember. Remember where you have been. Remember what your life looked like before. Remember the challenges that God got you through. Maybe you are not where you want to be yet. But perhaps today you can still be thankful that you are not where you used to be.

And if you are currently in a deep pit right now, you can hold onto the hope given to us in Matthew 6:33. If we keep seeking God with all our heart, He will provide. Just cling to

Him and don't let go. He will pull you up out of that pit. He will make everything work out for good. I have been there. I have been buried deep in a hole of depression and anxiety. I have been through some mighty rough days. But God got me through them. So I know firsthand that there is always hope. He pulled me out of the darkness. And He can do the same for you.

Maybe you are not where you want to be yet.
But perhaps today you can still be thankful
that you are not where you used to be.

Daily Reflection

Is there anything in your life that you are hoping for? Does it feel like you are never going to get what you want?

Can you look back on your life and be thankful for where you are now? And can you trust God to work out whatever it is you are struggling with?

_____

_____

_____

_____

_____

Evening Reflection

Write down five things that you are thankful for.

_____

_____

_____

_____

_____

_____

_____

_____

Day 15

Yes, you will be enriched in every way so that you can always be generous. And when we take your gifts to those who need them, they will thank God.

— 2 Corinthians 9:11

My husband loves to plant vegetables. Twice a year he will till up the garden, and plant a variety of seeds. He fertilizes the garden and makes sure the soil gets the right nutrients. Every day he is faithful to water the garden, dispose of any weeds, and ensure that the scarecrows are doing their job. He loyally nourishes this plot of land and makes sure it gets the best care.

Before long, we will begin to see little sprouts. And over time they will each grow into full size plants. It's amazing how a miniscule seed can turn into a flourishing plant. But all of my husband's hard work pays off, and we often have so many vegetables that we have to give some away.

Gratitude is a lot like having a garden. When we practice gratitude, we are planting seeds. We might start off with the smallest seed there is, but we have to be faithful and keep watering it. We have to be faithful and keep feeding our minds the right nutrients. Then over time we will begin to harvest hope, joy, faith, and love.

I noticed this in my own life. Times when I let gratitude slide, I can see a direct correlation in my life. Things around me seemed gloomier. My relationships seemed off balance. And I felt disconnected from God. But when I continued practicing gratitude, my outlook was better, my relationships improved, and my walk with God deepened as well. It's amazing how the more we appreciate things, the more there is to appreciate.

When we practice gratitude, we are planting seeds. Over time we will begin to harvest hope, joy, faith, and love.

Daily Reflection

Have you ever planted anything (literally or figuratively) and watched it grow?

How did you feel when the fruits of your labor paid off?

Evening Reflection

Write down five things that you are thankful for.

Part 3

Gratitude and Your
Relationships with Others

Day 16

And we know God causes everything to work together for the good of those who love God and are called according to his purpose for them.

– Romans 8:28

A few years ago, my husband and I were on our way home from the mountains when we decided to do a little hiking. This was before we had a GPS or a smartphone, so my husband handed me the map and asked me to direct him toward a particular mountain. It went well for a while, until my husband decided to make a spontaneous right hand turn. My immediate response was to panic, just knowing that we were going to get lost. My husband continued making haphazard turns. Or so it seemed. To my amazement, we arrived at a state park.

At this park there were several hiking trails to choose from, so we went in the ranger station to ask for advice on a good trail. But the ranger and another rambler were talking for quite some time, and didn't seem to notice that there were other people around. So we left the ranger station and randomly picked a trail close to where we parked. After we had been walking for a while, we passed a man who was descending the mountain. In his usual friendly nature, my husband briefly spoke to the man, and then we continued on our way. When we got to the top of the mountain, we were rewarded with an extraordinary view. But we didn't stay on the mountaintop long, for we felt an unexplainable urgency to leave.

As we traveled back down the trail, we met up with the same man again. This time he was lying on a bench, so we stopped to ask him if he was ok. We were shocked when he said that he had climbed the mountain to end his life. My husband and I glanced at each other for a moment, trying to think of the right words to say to this hurting man.

We tried to tell him that his friends and family wouldn't want to see him go. But he said that he didn't have any loved ones. So we then told the man that God wouldn't want him to end his life. Sadly, the man said that he didn't believe in God. So we tried to explain that God wanted to be there for him in his time of trouble, if he would allow it. And we also said that we felt God brought us to him in that moment.

The man seemed to listen to what we said, and we prayed that our words were absorbed. Finally, we parted ways as the man remained on the bench. We walked at a normal pace for a bit. Then when we were out of range, we ran to the ranger station and told them what happened. They thanked us for letting them know, and they immediately made their way up the trail to the lonely man.

If we learn to live with our arms open wide, God will take our hand and guide our steps. And we will discover that His plan was so much greater than ours. I now thank God for being our pilot that day. Numerous things did not go according to our plan. If we did not decide to go hiking, if my husband did not make a random turn, if we did not choose the trail that we did, and if we had tarried on the mountaintop, we would not have had the opportunity to help this man. I pray that our words made an impact and that this man allowed God to help heal his broken heart. Often times in life, we get discouraged when things don't go how we think that they should. But if we trust God to be our pilot, He will lead us to the right place at the right time.

If we learn to live with our arms open wide, God will take our hand and guide our steps. And we will discover that His plan was so much greater than ours.

Daily Reflection

Can you think of a time when things did not go according to plan, but looking back it seemed like divine intervention?

_____

_____

_____

_____

Take a moment to thank God for guiding your steps.

_____

_____

_____

_____

_____

Evening Reflection

Write down five things that you are thankful for.

_____

_____

_____

_____

_____

_____

_____

Day 17

I have not stopped thanking God for you. I pray for you constantly.

– Ephesians 1:16

At my previous place of employment, we had something called Star Cards. Employees would give them to each other as a way of saying "good job" or "thank you" for any number of things. If a colleague helped one of their fellow coworkers with a project, a Star Card might be given. Or if an employee put in a lot of extra time at work to ensure a particular task was completed, the person might receive a Star Card from their manager.

One thing I noticed with those Star Cards - they always brought a smile. People feel good when they are appreciated. Even if they are just doing their job, they like to know that they matter. They like to know that they make a difference. It gives them a sense of purpose. It doesn't take much time at all to express our gratitude towards someone, but the words "thank you" universally speak to all hearts.

Similarly, last February my coworkers decided to have a little Valentine's fun. Everyone was asked to hang a gift bag on their cubicle wall. Then each team member would go around and fill one another's bags with Valentines (the little cards that children hand out at school) or candy. And we were also asked to write down something that we appreciated about each other and place that in the corresponding person's gift bag as well. When Valentine's Day came, we all had a heart-warming time reading what our teammates wrote. It was something so simple, yet it brought smiles to our faces.

Too often we get in a hurry and go about our day without taking the time to express our gratitude towards each other. Saying thank you only takes one moment. But that one moment can ultimately express so much meaning.

The words "thank you" universally speak to all hearts.

Daily Reflection

Do you remember a time when someone thanked you for a job well done? How did it make you feel?

Is there someone you can thank today?

Evening Reflection

Write down five things that you are thankful for.

Day 18

Be thankful in all circumstances, for this is God's will for you who belong to Christ Jesus.

— 1 Thessalonians 5:18

One afternoon, I boarded a plane with three of my coworkers to head home after a conference in Boston. For some reason, none of our seats were together. So I found my seat and sat down next to a lady with downcast eyes.

The lady looked up and began to talk. But she didn't stop. In fact, she talked to me the entire flight back to Florida. She told me about her son who had been killed in the Middle East. She told me about her daughter who had a baby at fourteen. She told me about her grandchild who she had legal custody of, since her daughter was just too young to be a mom. She told me about her husband and his line of work.

By the time we landed in Florida, I knew this lady's whole life. But this was a different lady than the one who I first sat next to. This lady now had hope in her eyes. She thanked me for being there during the flight. She even wore a smile now.

This lady was thankful for one small thing - my time to lend a listening ear. And that one small thing may have helped heal her broken heart. Our time is a precious gift that we can give to those around us. There are so many hurting, lonely people in this world. So many of us just need someone to hear us, someone to understand us. It didn't cost me anything to listen to this lady's story. But it meant the world to her.

Our time is a precious gift that we can freely give to those around us.

Daily Reflection

Can you think of someone who is in need of a friend or a listening ear?

_____

_____

_____

_____

_____

If so, will you consider scheduling a coffee date with that person?

Evening Reflection

Write down five things that you are thankful for.

Day 19

Every time I think of you, I give thanks to my God.

– Philippians 1:3

"Thanks for all you do." That is something that my husband and I often say to one another. We might say this in person, or we might text it during the day. It only takes one second, but it shows a mountain of appreciation. It is an all-encompassing statement for things that we each do, because we know that sometimes we forget to show our thanks for the big and the little things alike.

It is important to extend our gratitude toward the people in our lives. Say "thank you" to the cashier at the grocery store. If a coworker helps you with a project, express your thanks. If your spouse unloads the dishwasher, tell him or her you appreciate it. If your child takes out the trash, say "thank you."

Our gratitude can help boost someone's day. In fact, it will make that person want to do more. For example, if your child is often behind on chores, showing them your appreciation will help make that task less daunting. And they just might do their chores quicker. Why? Because everyone likes to know that they are appreciated and that they matter.

You never know how the words "thank you" might brighten someone's day. Let me share an example from my own life. One day I felt led to share a Bible verse with a friend. But when I did so, I was hesitant, no longer sure if this was the right thing. I did so anyway, and then went about my day wondering about it. Later on, she told me how much it meant to her. She said that before she left her house that morning, she glanced at her dusty Bible, thinking that she needed to get back into her studies. And then I gave her that Bible verse which had hit home. This one small incident showed me the importance of expressing our thanks. If my friend had not done so, it probably would have kept me from reaching out in the future. So as you go about your day today, look for people who you can say those two words to.

You never know how the words "thank you" might brighten someone's day.

Daily Reflection

Who can you say "thank you" to today?

Can you think of someone in your life who might need your friendship today? If so, what is one small thing you can do to show that person you care?

_____

_____

_____

_____

_____

Evening Reflection

Write down five things that you are thankful for.

_____

_____

_____

_____

_____

_____

Day 20

Let the message about Christ, in all its richness, fill your lives. Teach and counsel each other with all the wisdom he gives. Sing psalms and hymns and spiritual songs to God with thankful hearts.

– Colossians 3:16

One night I was in the kitchen making dinner, prepping lunch for the next day, washing fruit, and so on. My husband came into the kitchen and asked me what he could do to help. I told him, "Nothing. Just go about your biz." But my husband's reply was, "You are my biz!"

We both laughed. But this made me think - how often do we show our loved ones that they are our "biz" or business. Because in the end this ultimately speaks our appreciation. We might say the words "thank you" to them at times. But expressing gratitude is not only saying the words. It is also showing it with our actions.

Take time to help your spouse with one of their daily tasks. You can help fix their lunch to take to work. Or have coffee waiting for them when they get up in the morning. Instead of telling your children to clean up their room, maybe you could do it with them and they will have more fun in the process. Or after they have finished their homework, maybe you could play a game together. Consider taking time out of your busy day to eat lunch with a friend, instead of saying in passing that you need to get together. Or call that person who you haven't touched based with in a while.

Life can be stressful. But when we take time to be there for each other, we can help ease burdens and lift spirits. And when we find time to help others, this will lift our own spirits as well.

I have seen this in my own life. One small example - I like to post inspirational quotes on social media. Sometimes someone will respond with something like, "I needed to hear that today." Knowing that I can help give someone else a bit of encouragement to get through their day brings me a bit of joy too.

Expressing gratitude is not only saying the words. It is also showing it with our actions.

Daily Reflection

Think of a way you can show your family that they are your biz!

_____

_____

_____

What is one thing you can do for a loved one today?

_____

_____

_____

_____

_____

Evening Reflection

Write down five things that you are thankful for.

_____

_____

_____

_____

_____

Part 4

Gratitude and Your
Relationship with God

Day 21

Let all that I am praise the Lord; may I never forget the good things he does for me.

– Psalm 103:2

A couple of years ago, I interviewed for a job that I thought I wanted. It would have meant a change in my career, since I didn't have any knowledge or skill to get me started. But I liked the fact that it was at a local college because I would get summers off and a break around Christmas as well. The people who I dealt with at the interview seemed nice. And most importantly it was close to home. I prayed that God would help me get this job.

I didn't hear anything from them for a number of weeks. So I contacted the administrative assistant in the department and she told me that it was still up in the air. So I waited and prayed some more. Then about three months after my interview, I called again. This time I was told that the position was given to another candidate who had the experience which I was lacking.

I felt disappointed when I heard the news. And I wondered why God didn't answer my prayer. Why didn't He help me to get this job? It would have been "perfect." Or so I thought.

Fast forward another three months. This time I landed a different job. A better job. One that I loved. I already had the experience, so I didn't have to start from scratch. My new team was awesome to work with. Many of them felt like instant friends. And the benefits were better than the other job.

I am honestly glad that things worked out the way they did. I believe God knew what He was doing. When you live in gratitude, you will begin to see that times when you did not get what you hoped for, it was really God working behind the scenes for something better to come into your life. Looking back, I thought I was disappointed about not getting the first job. But in reality it now seems as though I was just disappointed about not getting a six-mile commute!

Times when you did not get what you hoped for, it was really God working behind the scenes for something better to come into your life.

Daily Reflection

Can you name a time when you were disappointed by an unanswered prayer?

If so, can you see now that this might have been a blessing in disguise?

Evening Reflection

Write down five things that you are thankful for.

Day 22

Give thanks to the Lord, for he is good! His faithful love endures forever.

– Psalm 107:1

One particular Friday I boarded an airplane completely exhausted. It had been a rough week, to say the least. I had worked late every night and got up early each morning. I was so depleted that I fell asleep before the plane even took off! I never fall asleep on airplanes, because I don't feel comfortable sleeping while a stranger is sitting next to me. So this was definitely a bizarre incident.

If you've been on an airplane, then you know that before you take off, the flight attendants go through a series of important guidelines in case of an emergency. I dozed in and out as they talked about oxygen masks and floating cushions.

Then to my dismay, I heard one of the ladies say, "For those of you who weren't paying attention, we're going to do this all over again." And they did! The flight attendants went through the whole routine a second time. To this day I wonder if it was because they saw me sleeping. Maybe they wanted to give me a second chance to pay attention and take in the safety instructions.

I laugh about this story now. But it made me think. God gives us second chances every single day. Every day when we wake up, we have another chance to get things right, another chance to fix our mistakes, another chance to make an impact on someone, another chance to love our family, and another chance to honor God. And that is something we can all be thankful for!

God gives us second chances every single day.

Daily Reflection

Can you think of a time when you needed a second chance?

_____

_____

_____

_____

_____

Did you capitalize on the opportunity? How did it turn out? If you didn't capitalize on it, perhaps it's not too late?

_____

_____

_____

_____

_____

Evening Reflection

Write down five things that you are thankful for.

_____

_____

_____

_____

_____

_____

_____

_____

Day 23

So they rolled the stone aside. Then Jesus looked up to heaven and said, "Father, thank you for hearing me. You always hear me, but I said it out loud for the sake of all these people standing here, so that they will believe you sent me." Then Jesus shouted, "Lazarus, come out!"

– John 11:41-43

There is a Bible story that you might be familiar with. Jesus was friends with three siblings - Lazarus and his two sisters Mary and Martha. Lazarus had become ill, so Mary and Martha sent word for Jesus. I am sure that the sisters had hoped that Jesus would come straight to them and heal Lazarus. But He didn't. In fact, Lazarus died and Jesus didn't make it to them until four days after his death. But the story doesn't end there. When Jesus returned, He went to Lazarus' tomb and raised him from the dead. No doubt Jesus allowed Lazarus to die in order to help non-believers see the glory of God.

But there is something very important that I noticed in the Bible verse at the top of the page. Jesus gave thanks to God. Looking at the life of Jesus, we can see that there are many times when He gave thanks to God. The life of Jesus shows us how important it is to give thanks.

If Jesus gave thanks, how much more important is it for us to give thanks? It only takes one second to do, but do we often overlook it? And when we do forget to express our thanks, I wonder how God feels about our seemingly ungrateful attitude. Or what if we actually prayed about something and then forgot to give thanks when things turned out well. I know I have been guilty of this myself. But I hope that this new path will help us to be more mindful of giving thanks in the future.

The life of Jesus shows us how important it is to give thanks.

Daily Reflection

When God sends good things your way, do you say a prayer of thanks?

Or have there been times when you actually prayed about something and then forgot to give thanks when things turned out well?

Evening Reflection

Write down five things that you are thankful for.

Day 24

Seek his will in all you do, and he will show you which path to take.

– Proverbs 3:6

When my husband and I travel from Florida to the mountains, we like taking the back roads for part of the way. It is a lot more pleasant if we can avoid that Atlanta traffic. There is one particular spot that we pass through which we call five points. The first time we encountered the intersection, we almost turned down the wrong road. There are two left turns next to each other; we almost took the first left turn, but the second one was the one we needed.

On one particular trip, when we were coming home from the mountains, we plugged the route into the smartphone and went on our merry way. We decided to make a quick stop along the way, but got back on the road before too long. After we were driving for a while, I realized that the not-so-smartphone recalculated our route when we stopped. And we were now heading toward Atlanta! My normal reflex was to panic. But I tried my best to keep cool and turn the situation over to God. I thanked Him ahead of time for getting us back on track.

We still carry an Atlas around with us, so my husband asked me to look for a town on the map that was east of Macon, GA and plug that into the GPS. Macon is where we switch over from back roads to the interstate on our way home. So as my husband suggested I looked at the map and picked the town that seemed to be closest to Macon, and put that in the app on the phone. We actually wound up having a nice drive along the way, seeing different scenery. I thanked God for this pleasant ride with my husband. And then we couldn't believe it when we turned up at the very same five points, coming in on the road that we almost accidentally took that first time. This taught me a valuable lesson about making gratitude a way of life. Even when we take a wrong turn in life, God will still bring us back to where we need to be.

Even when we take a wrong turn in life,
God will still bring us back to where we need to be.

Daily Reflection

Have you ever taken a wrong turn in life (literally or figuratively) and God still led you back on the right path?

_____

_____

_____

Looking back on this incident, does it help alter your outlook?

_____

_____

_____

_____

Evening Reflection

Write down five things that you are thankful for.

_____

_____

_____

_____

_____

Day 25

And give thanks for everything to God the Father in the name of our Lord Jesus Christ.

– Ephesians 5:20

When you give someone a gift, doesn't it bring you pleasure to know that the recipient loved the item? As the saying goes, it is better to give than to receive. It often brings the giver just as much joy, if not more, as the receiver. Imagine if it was your child and you got them that toy that they really, really wanted? Isn't it fun to see them tear open the package with excitement?

Now imagine giving someone a gift, but you can tell that they don't like it. Or worse, they might say something like, "I don't like pink." Or, "This is ... interesting." You can read it all over their face that it is not at all what they were hoping for. Or they think it is just plain ghastly. That would make you feel bad, right? I know it sure would make me feel bad.

Now let's imagine that the one giving the gift is God and we are the recipients. He showers us with a multitude of blessings each and every day. But often times we hurry on our way and forget to say thanks. We are God's children. He loves us beyond belief. And He wants to see us happy. He showers us with blessings every single day. So could it be that our gratitude is a gift to God? Maybe when we express our appreciation, it brings God joy. Imagine how it must feel to Him when we say two simple words, "Thank you."

Our gratitude is a gift to God.

Daily Reflection

Have you ever given someone a gift that was not well received? If so, how did it make you feel?

Do you sometimes forget to thank God for the gifts in your life? If so, take a moment now to show Him your appreciation.

Evening Reflection

Write down five things that you are thankful for.

Day 26

You are worthy, O Lord our God, to receive glory and honor and power. For you created all things, and they exist because you created what you pleased.

– Revelation 4:11

My dogs love when my husband or I sit on the floor. They immediately get in our laps, and might even smother us with kisses. Not long ago, I was thinking about this and wondering why they enjoy it so much. Perhaps it is because we came down to their level. Maybe they always feel like we are way up high, as they look at us from the floor. So coming down to their level, they can finally interact with us.

This made me think about God being way up high, seemingly out of reach, as we go about our business here on earth. We cannot see Him, so it can be difficult for us to grasp His presence. But the truth is that God always comes down to our level. He meets us wherever we are. We could be in the deepest valley and He will be there to help us out. We could be on the highest mountain and He is there pulling us higher.

Walking in gratitude can help us find true contentment in life. We will begin to see that just because we don't always feel God's presence doesn't mean that He isn't there. He is always there, right beside us, holding our hand, if only we allow Him to. And when we walk in gratitude, we will begin to see this more and more in our lives. Walking in gratitude will help us to even out the valleys and peaks we go through in life. We will still have troubles at times. That is inevitable. But even when we do have troubles, we can remain at peace because of the One who is constantly beside us.

Walking in gratitude can help us find true contentment in life.

Daily Reflection

Where are you right now in your life? Deep in a valley or high on a mountaintop? Or maybe somewhere in between?

_____

_____

_____

_____

_____

Whatever the case may be, take a moment to ask God to meet you right where you are.

_____

_____

_____

_____

_____

Evening Reflection

Write down five things that you are thankful for.

_____

_____

_____

_____

_____

_____

_____

_____

_____

Day 27

Don't worry about anything; instead, pray about everything. Tell God what you need, and thank him for all he has done.

– Philippians 4:6

Life can be stressful. We all have a multitude of projects on our plates. Our daily routine is a balancing act of things we need to get done for our family, work, home, church, and so on.

Then we turn on the news and see many stories of death and destruction. It seems to get worse every day. These things can bring us down if we let them. But they don't have to! We have an awesome God by our side each and every day. He can see us through the hard times.

I have had days when I felt like I was in quicksand. I struggled to pull myself out. But then a dump truck would come along and drop more muck on top of me. Getting out seemed hopeless. But the problem was that I was relying on my own strength, instead of God's strength.

God is always, always, always there. We just have to call out to Him and He will be more than happy to help. That is what

He wants above all else - to be a part of our lives. But we have to allow Him to be there, instead of trying to do it all on our own.

Some days I still get overwhelmed. And if I stop and think about it, I will realize that I took back control. I was trying to do everything on my own. Again. I have to relinquish control to God. And I have to remind myself that no one and nothing can stop God's plans. God's plans cannot be thwarted (Job 42:2). So what is there to worry about? He will always work everything out.

Whatever you are going through today, hand God the reigns. Allow Him to take care of your worries. No matter what is weighing you down, He can handle it. After all, He created the whole world! So I am sure He can handle anything that you are going through.

No one and nothing can stop God's plans.
So what is there to worry about?

Daily Reflection

Write down all the things that are worrying you.

_____

_____

_____

Now take a moment to ask God to help you with each one of those things.

_____

_____

_____

_____

Evening Reflection

Write down five things that you are thankful for.

_____

_____

_____

_____

Day 28

Wherever your treasure is, there the desires of your heart will also be.

– Matthew 6:21

One thing that has helped me on this journey is spending time with God each day. If you start your morning with the Lord, this will help set the tone for the day. Prayer and Bible reading first thing really help start each day off on the right foot.

Some people find reading the Bible to be overwhelming. Many times this boils down to two obstacles that the enemy puts in our way.

First, we might think the Bible is hard to understand. In order to overcome this, I found a Bible translation that was easy to understand. In this book, I have used New Living Translation (NLT). But there are many Bible translations available. I recommend going to a book store and browsing through the different options until you find one you are comfortable with.

The second obstacle that the enemy puts in our path when we attempt to read the Bible, is that our minds wander. I still struggle with this at times. One thing that helps me is to read the Bible in the morning, before the day's troubles have had a chance to crowd my brain. It helps to be in a quiet room without distractions. And when I am done reading, I try to summarize in my head what I read. If I can't summarize it, then I know I wasn't paying attention. So I will go back and read it again.

But you might be wondering how reading the Bible will help with gratitude. When we read the Bible, we are allowing God's Word to sink deep into our souls. His Word is getting in our hearts and in our minds. If we fill ourselves up with the right things, then there will be less room inside of us for the bad things, like negativity and complaining. We have to be intentional about igniting passion on the inside of ourselves. And that begins with God and His word.

If you start your morning with the Lord, this will help set the tone for the day.

Daily Reflection

If you have a Bible, take a moment to open it and read from it today.

_____

_____

_____

If you don't have a Bible, maybe you will consider taking a trip to the book store to purchase one this week?

_____

_____

_____

_____

Evening Reflection

Write down five things that you are thankful for.

_____

_____

_____

_____

Day 29

There is no greater love than to lay down one's life for one's friends.

– John 15:13

If you have accepted Jesus into your life, then you know what an awesome gift we have. We were all born sinners and deserve to perish. But God loved us so much, that He sent His Son to die for us. Jesus paid the penalty of death for us. There is no way we could have achieved salvation on our own. And there is no way we could ever repay Jesus for what He did. But we don't have to. It was a gift from God. Because that is the kind of Father He is. He loves us so much that He wanted to save us. And ultimately He wants to spend eternity with us.

And He loves us so much that He is with us each and every day. No matter what we are going through, He is there. If we call out to Him, He will answer. If we need a friend, He is there. If we need a comforter, He is there. If we need acceptance, He is there. If we need love, He is there. It fills me with awe to think about how much He loves all of His children. And because of His love, I think it is especially important to express gratitude towards God every day for all the blessings in our lives, and most importantly for Jesus.

But the first step is to accept this free gift. So if you have not yet accepted Jesus into your life, I invite you to read the prayer in the back of the book.

Express gratitude towards God every day for all the blessings in our lives, and most importantly for Jesus.

Daily Reflection

Have you accepted Jesus into your life?

_____

_____

_____

_____

_____

If the answer to the question above was "yes" - take a moment to thank Him for dying on the cross. If the answer to the question above was "no" - is there something that is holding you back?

_____

_____

_____

_____

_____

Evening Reflection

Write down five things that you are thankful for.

_____

_____

_____

_____

_____

_____

_____

_____

_____

Part 5

Conclusion

Day 30

Give thanks to the Lord, for he is good! His faithful love endures forever.

– Psalm 136:1

Congratulations! You made it to day thirty. Now what? Should we lay down our gratitude, like we are laying down our fork after dinner?

No! We are just getting started. Gratitude is a habit that we are just beginning to learn. So we must keep pressing forward on this new path.

I have learned a lot over the last thirty days. And I bet you have too. Take a moment to pause and think about what your month looked like. My days were filled with good things and not so good things, just like always. And I bet yours were too.

But it all boils down to this - gratitude is a decision we have to make every day. When those not so good things happen, we can choose how we will react to them. Will we get upset because things didn't go our way? Or will we stop and realize that even though there were some things going wrong, there were still an awful lot of things going right?

I know life can be hard. But each and every day God gives us so much. We wake up each morning, fresh breath in our lungs, and a new day to live life. When we stop and take notice that is when the miracles begin to take place. That is when we will begin to find true contentment in life. That is when we will begin to harvest peace, faith, love, and joy.

During this gratitude challenge, when I focused on the good things, I didn't have room for the bad things. I couldn't feel both good and bad at the same time. If something went wrong, my normal reaction was to feel irritated, annoyed, upset, angry, or some other negative emotion. But if I stopped and focused on the blessings in my life, I would feel happy, at peace, and content. Eventually the good feelings overrode the negative feelings.

And personally I would much rather feel happy than not. So that is why I choose to keep going. I am excited to see what else lies ahead on this path. And I hope you will join me. Whatever you decide, please remember one thing - *Every Day is a Gift!*

Gratitude is a decision we have to make every day.

Daily Reflection

What did you learn over the last thirty days?

Do you plan to continue on this new path?

Evening Reflection

Write down five things that you are thankful for.

Accepting Jesus into Your Life

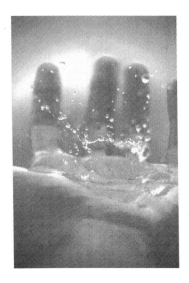

Do you have a personal relationship with God? If not, then I invite you to do so today. I promise you that you will not regret it. Having a relationship with God will bring comfort and peace into your life.

But having a relationship with God, starts with accepting Jesus. The Bible says that we are all sinners and fall short of the glory of God (Romans 3:23). We all deserve to perish (Romans 6:23). And there is nothing we can do on our own to achieve salvation (Ephesians 2:9).

But the good news is that "If you openly declare that Jesus is Lord and believe in your heart that God raised him from the dead, you will be saved" (Romans 10:9). This is because

Jesus paid the price that we could never pay. He died for all of our sins. He took them on Himself so that we might have eternal life. Then three days after Jesus' death, He rose from the dead. This ultimately defeated death and gave us the hope of salvation.

A life with Jesus by your side can be so freeing. Every day we struggle with the weight of the world on our shoulders. But it doesn't have to be that way. We can accept Jesus into our hearts, and let God handle our troubles. If you believe this, I invite you to pray this prayer now.

Lord Jesus, I ask You to please forgive me of my sins. I believe that You died on the cross for me and rose from the grave three days later. I can never thank You enough for paying my sin debt. Thank You for hearing my prayer. Thank You for Your unconditional love. I am ready to hand my life over to You. I am ready to walk in Your strength and power. I am ready for You to be the center, purpose, and meaning in my life. I am ready for you to be my Lord and Savior. In Jesus' name I pray, amen.

If you prayed this prayer - Congratulations! I would love to hear from you. Please contact me at www.bridgetathomas.com/contact/.

Notes

1. Taken from *Same Kind of Different as Me*, by Ron Hall and Denver Moore, © 2006 by Ron Hall. Used by permission of Thomas Nelson. www.thomasnelson.com.

Acknowledgements

First and foremost, I want to thank Jesus, for the gift of salvation. And for bringing peace into my life, and for helping me share it with others. I could not have done any of this without Him.

I want to thank my husband, Mickey. You were always cheering me on when I talked about my dream of writing. And you taught me a lot about integrity, always doing the right thing, and always helping others. When we learn to help others, this in turn brings gratitude into our own lives. Thank you for your love, support, and patience on this journey. You mean the world to me. I love you forever!

I want to thank my parents and my sisters who encouraged me to write ever since I wrote my first book at twelve years old. Thank you for your love and support. And thank you for walking with me through the gratitude challenge, when I first ventured out and shared it with the world. I love you guys!

I also want to thank my launch team. It was such a blessing and an honor that you were happy and willing to help. I truly appreciate it, more than you will ever know!

Thank you to my editor and cover designer, Stacey. You were a blessing to me as I went through this process. Thank you so very much for all your help, for answering all my zany questions, and for ultimately being my sounding board. You helped me with a lot more than you originally signed up for!

And thank you to my friend, Chris, for helping me with a final proofread. You are such a sweet friend and a blessing in my life!

And a big thank you to all of my family and friends for being there. Whether you knew it or not, you played a part in this, as I learned the value of gratitude.

About the Author

Bridget's passion is to help people learn to live freely in Jesus. She feels that Christians who have been set free, still live as though they are trapped. And her calling is to motivate Christians to break out of those chains. Bridget knows that she needs a whole lot of grace from Jesus, every single day. And she encourages others to find that grace as well.

Bridget loves reading in her spare time, and is a fan of classic literature. She enjoys traveling, crocheting, and watching college baseball and softball games. And she is particularly fond of looking for black bears in the Great Smoky Mountains. Bridget lives in Florida with her husband.

For more information or to contact Bridget, please visit her website at www.bridgetathomas.com.

One Final Thing

Dear Friend,

Thank you for reading this book! I truly hope you enjoyed it and got some meaning out of it. I really would appreciate your feedback. So would you please take a moment to leave a review on Amazon and let me know what you thought? Thank you so much!

Every Day is a Gift!

Bridget A. Thomas